TWO WORDS FOR SNOW

TWO WORDS FOR SNOW

Richard Sanger

Red Deer PRESS

Published by
Red Deer Press
Trailer C
2500 University Drive N.W.
Calgary Alberta Canada T2n 1N4
www.reddeerpress.com

Credits
Edited for the Press by Joyce Doolittle
Copyedited by Dennis Johnson
Cover design by Elliott Smith
Text design by Erin Woodward
Cover photo of Lucy Idlout courtesy of John Lauener
Printed and bound in Canada by Friesens for Red Deer Press

Acknowledgments
Financial support provided by the Canada Council, the Government of Canada through
the Book Publishing Industry Development Program (BPIDP), and the Alberta
Foundation for the Arts, a beneficiary of the Lottery Fund of the Government of Alberta.

National Library of Canada Cataloguing in Publication
Sanger, Richard, 1960–
Two words for snow / Richard Sanger.
A play.
First published: Toronto : PUC Play Service, 1999.
ISBN 0-88995-310-4
1. Peary, Robert E., 1856-1920--Drama. 2. North Pole--Discovery and
exploration--American--Drama. I. Title.
PS8587.A3723T86 2005   C812'.54   C2005-902478-X

For Matthew Sanger,

So many expeditions together,

And for Ted Chamberlin,

Who was there at the start.

Acknowledgements

For their generosity, insight and navigational expertise, many thanks to:

Alberta Theatre Projects, John Ball and the English Department at the Universiy of New Brunswick, the Banff Playwrights Colony, Maury Breslow and the Herman Voaden National Playwrighting Competition, the late Ron Bryden, Naomi Campbell, Joyce Doolittle, the late Bill Glassco, the late Urjo Kareda, Deborah Lambie, Laidlaw Foundation, Ross Manson, Andy McKim, Neil Munro, Vanessa Porteous, Chris Ralling, Clyde Sanger, Penny Sanger, Shaw Festival, Ricardo Sternberg, Tarragon Theatre, Colin Taylor, Theatre Passe Muraille, Thousand Islands Playhouse, Toronto Arts Council, Volcano Thatre, Craig Walker, Bob White.

We read in the *Negro Explorer*: "never for an instant does the odor or appearance of an Esquimo's habitation suggest the rose or geranium. The aroma of an East Side lunchroom is more like it" and must reflect immeadiately that . . . Akatingwah lay skin to skin with Henson, mingling the human smells of Greenland and America. A lost intimacy hides beneath the lines. Did bed abolish hierarchy, or only prove how closely it clings in a close embrace?

–Francis Spufford,
Times Literary Supplement, May 1992.

. . . the tribe in bondage learned to fortify itself by cunning assimilation of the religion of the Old World. What seemed to be surrender was redemption. What seemed the loss of tradition was its renewal. What seemed the death of faith was its rebirth. [. . .] What was captured from the captor was his God, for the subject African had come to the New World in an elemental intimacy with nature, with a profounder terror of blasphemy than the exhausted, hypocritcal Christian. [. . .] It is the beginning of the poetry of the New World. And the language used is, like the religion, that of the conqueror of the God. But the slave had wrested God from his captor.

–Derek Walcott,
"The Muse of History," 1974.

Production History

Two Words for Snow was first produced by Alberta Theatre Projects as part of the Pan-Canadian playRites '99 festival in Calgary, Alberta, January and February 1999. The cast was as follows:

Matthew Henson . . . Nigel Shawn Williams
Robert Peary Jr. . . . Edward Bélanger
Captain Bob Bartlett . . . Allan Morgan
Commander Robert Edwin Peary . . . William Webster
John Verhoeff . . . Philip Warren Sarsons
Dr. Franz Boas . . . Christopher Hunt
Akatingwah . . . Mieko Ouchi

Director . . . **Bob White**
Dramaturge . . . **Vanessa Porteous**
Set . . . **Scott Reid**
Costumes . . . **Judith Bowden**
Lighting . . . **Brian Pincott**
Assistant Designer . . . **Kim Stewart**
Music . . . **Kevin McGugan**

This revised version of the play (which eliminated one character and tightened several scenes) was produced by Volcano Theatre in Toronto, Ontario, January 2003, with the following cast:

Matthew Henson . . . Nigel Shawn Williams
Robert Peary Jr. . . . Tom Barnett
Captain Bob Bartlett . . . Hugh Thompson
Commander Robert Edwin Peary . . . David Fox
Dr. Franz Boas . . . Jerry Franken
Akatingwah . . . Lucy Idlout

Director . . . **Ross Manson**
Set and Costume Design . . . **Teresa Przybylski**
Lighting . . . **Bonnie Beecher**
Music . . . **John Gzowski**
Stage Managing . . . **Kate MacDonnell**
Producer . . . **Timothy Luginbuhl**

This play is based on historical fact. Peary was accompanied by an African American named Matthew Henson on his polar expeditions, including his allegedly successful final 1909 trek; Henson learned to speak Inuktitut and served as Peary's interpreter on those expeditions; both men fathered children with Inuit women; Peary brought back six Inuit to be put on display at the American Museum of Natural History; when four of them fell ill and eventually died, Henson served as an interpreter for the museum's director, the influential anthropologist Franz Boas, whose 1911 book, *The Handbook of North American Indian Languages,* first speculated on the number of Inuit words for snow.

These facts and others, and my characters' names are all historical; my play is a work of the imagination.

Characters

Matthew Henson, former assistant to Peary Sr., African American, 60 or so in 1935

Robert Peary Jr., engineer, white American, 25–35 in 1935

Captain Bob Bartlett, Newfoundland sea captain, late 30s in 1909

Commander Robert Edwin Peary (Piuli), explorer and naval officer, 50ish in 1909

Dr. Franz Boas, anthropologist, German Jewish origin, 60 or more in 1935

Akatingwah (Katie), Inuit, 17–20 in 1909

Setting

The Eskimo Room in the basement of the American Museum of Natural History, New York, 1935; and, in memory, aboard the *Roosevelt,* moored off the north shore of Ellesmere Island on the Peary North Pole Expedition, February 1909 and, later, in the Explorers Club, New York, Fall 1910.

Act One
1935:
Welcome to the Eskimo Room

The Eskimo Room in the basement of the American Museum of Natural History in New York. It is undergoing renovations. Henson, now in his 60s, is dressed in the uniform of his former employer, the Customs Office, and seated on a chair facing the audience. The uniform gives the impression, which he is happy to perpetuate, that he is an employee of the museum. Around him are cases covered with various drop cloths. Outside, it is a sweltering summer day; inside, everything seems varnished and nineteenth century. Footsteps are heard.

Peary Jr enters from behind.

Peary Jr: Mr. Henson? Mr. Henson? *(Pause. Sees him)* We met a long time ago. I'm Bob Peary—Junior. *(Pause)* The son of. Son of Commander Peary. *(Pause)* Do you hear me? The son of Commander Peary.

Pause.

Henson: Who?

Peary Jr: Commander Robert Edwin Peary.

Henson: Peary? Never heard of him.

Peary Jr: You are Mr. Henson?

Henson: Henson! Who's that now, son? *(Imperceptible chuckle)* Henson! Peary! Who are they?

Peary Jr: I'm looking for Matthew Henson. He went to the North Pole with my father.

Pause.

Henson: The North Pole?

Peary Jr: Yes.

Henson: You patted the dog?

Peary Jr: What dog?

Henson: Over there.

Peary Jr: *(Pointing to a waist-high lump covered with a drop cloth)* This?

Henson: Yes. Pull that off.

> *Peary Jr does so and we see a meteorite.*

It's called the Dog. Go on, pat it.

Peary Jr: You are Mr. Henson?

Henson: Pat the dog.

Peary Jr gives in and pats the dog.

How'd that feel? Cold?

Peary Jr: Very cold.

Henson: Welcome to the Eskimo Room.

Peary Jr: It's not like I remember it.

Henson: No, Sir. They're re-doing everything, changing the exhibits. Getting up to date.

Peary Jr: So they are. It's a pity. *(Pause)* I went to Mr. Henson's house looking for him. His wife said he was here most afternoons. I'd never been to Harlem before.

Henson: So you're an explorer, too, are you?

Peary Jr: In a manner of speaking—

Henson: It smells. *(Pause)* Don't you find Harlem smells?

Peary Jr: Well, on a hot day like today, it's—

Henson: It's a problem with coloured people. You put too many of them together and they smell.

Peary Jr: Mr. Henson—

Henson: That's it. Congratulations! You've made a discovery.

Peary Jr: I saw the story in the paper. The interview you gave. *(Pause)* It said you got to the Pole before Father.

Henson: I was speculating, Mr. Peary. Just speculating.

Peary Jr: Speculating! Is that what you call it? Please think, Mr. Henson.

Henson: I never saw the story.

Peary Jr: Here it is. *(Hands him a paper)* Of course you only say these things when Father can't correct you—

Henson: Robert Edwin Peary: R. E. P.

Peary Jr: So it falls to me—

Henson: Robert Edwin Peary, Junior. Is that right?

Peary Jr: It falls to me, as usual, to defend Father's name. What did they pay you?

Henson: Pay me? Nothing. I was just trying to tell the truth.

Peary Jr: My father told Congress the truth. He swore on the Bible.

Henson: Yes, that was unusual—your father with his hand on the Bible!

Peary Jr: Congress, the National Geographic Society and the *New York Times* all verified Father's claim. And now you say these things and stir it all up again.

Henson: What do you want me to do?

Peary Jr: I'm sure your savings don't go very far.

Henson: The North Pole is plenty far.

Peary Jr: Mr. Henson, there's a journalist from the *New York Times* who is very interested in speaking to you, in hearing your story. The Peary family would like to help you—

Henson: Shhh!

Henson listens to something we can't hear.

Peary Jr: What was that?

Henson: Shhh. It was very peaceful in here a few minutes ago.

Peary Jr: Mr. Henson, the family understands you might feel—

Henson: Robert Edwin Peary. Rest in Peace.

Peary Jr: You—you haven't been treated well—

Henson: It's the Eskimo Room—

Peary Jr: I beg your pardon?

Henson: Where are the Eskimos? *(Laughs)*

Dogs Barking

Peary's study aboard the Roosevelt *on the north shore of Ellesmere Island. We hear a dog barking, then silence.*

Bartlett playing the pianola, singing the duet from The Beggar's Opera; *Henson enters, taking the female part.*

Bartlett: Were I laid on Greenland's coast
　　　　And in my arms embraced my lass,
　　　　Warm amidst eternal frost
　　　　Too soon my half year's light would pass.

Henson: *(entering and swooning about)*
　　　　Were I sold on Indian soil
　　　　Soon as the burning day was closed
　　　　I could mock the sultry toil
　　　　While on my charmer's breast reposed.

Henson lays his head on Bartlett's chest.

Bartlett: And I would love you all the day

Henson: Every night would kiss and play

Bartlett: If—

Bartlett notices Peary, who has just entered.

Henson: If with me you'd fondly—

Peary: If.

Henson: Commander, I was just—

Peary: If you please, Henson. There's work to do.

Henson: What?

Peary: We're not finished our research for Dr. Boas. Find the Eskimo.

Henson: Which one?

Peary: The girl. We've done all the others.

Exit Henson.

Bartlett: Commander Peary, I came down to see you and Henson was here—

Peary: He was cleaning my quarters, I believe.

Bartlett: We thought we'd sing a little air. Just to raise the spirits.

Peary: I went up on deck, Captain, because it was very quiet, and I didn't know why. Do you know why?

Bartlett: Because you couldn't hear us singing.

Peary: It's because we can't hear the dogs. Why are they quiet? It's your watch, Captain, your ship, and you don't know.

Bartlett: You hear a bark now and then.

Peary: They're dead. *(Pause)* Four of them were sick, some Eskie killed them, and now the others are—

Bartlett: Feeding?

Peary: That's right. Gnawing the bones.

Bartlett: Jesus, Mary and Joseph.

Peary: Or is it right? Do you think one dog should eat another, Captain?

Bartlett: It's not table manners—not in St. John's at least.

Peary: It's madness, that's what it is. Eating your own species. I stood up there and watched them do it. But all of this is madness and we have to go through with it. *(Abruptly)* Captain, I need you to calculate the rate the ice is drifting at—

Bartlett: Yes, I was thinking, Commander, it's like a tablecloth, right? We're setting off in the dark across a tablecloth that's moving—

Peary: I'll need to know the knots per day. The direction is probably south-south-easterly, but you'll need to verify that as well—degrees and minutes. Then we'll factor it all into our calculations. Understood?

Bartlett: Yes.

Peary: It's your watch, isn't it?

Bartlett: Aye.

> *Exit Bartlett. Peary takes out paper and pen, starts to write and stops. This is a letter he has been working on. Henson appears with Katie.*

Henson: She was sleeping. In their quarters. Akatingwah—that's her name.

Peary: And you call her Katie, don't you? Tell her the business. I've been writing to Bobby. I want to finish this sentence. . . . . *(He doesn't)*

Henson: *(Speaking English as Inuktitut)* Your husband is Qisuk and your father is Ootah. Is this right?

> *Katie nods.*

Now Ootah is going on the big hunting trip with Piuli. They are going to the Big Nail. To make the journey safe, you must take off your clothes for Piuli.

> *No response from Katie.*

It is very important that you take your clothes off.

> *No response.*

If you take your clothes off, you will have lots of children.

> *No response.*

And you and your children will be very healthy.

Peary: What are you telling her?

Henson: I'm explaining the scientific benefits.

Peary: Look at her. What is she—sixteen, seventeen? I can't tell with Eskies.

Katie: Why should I take off my clothes for Piuli?

Henson: Because Piuli says take your clothes off.

Katie: Does Piuli like me? Does he want me?

Peary: *(to Katie, digging out a candy)* Look!

Henson: Put it away, Sir.

Peary: It's just a caramel.

Henson: You'll ruin it.

Katie: What does Piuli want?

Peary: Then let's get on with it.

Henson: He wants you to take your clothes off. That's all.

Katie: He doesn't want me?

Henson: No, he just—

Katie: So no one wants me.

Henson: No, I—

Katie: You?

Henson: Yes, I—

Katie: Then let me take my clothes off.

Peary: Henson, could you hold this—

> *Peary hands Henson a large screen, Katie moves
> in front of the camera and seems about to remove
> her clothing, but as Peary ducks behind the camera
> and Henson arranges the screen, she suddenly
> vanishes.*

Peary: What! Where'd she go?

Henson: I'll find her.

Peary: No, no. We'll do her picture later. Never let an Eskie think you can't find another one to do their job. That's when your problems start.

Henson: Sir, I meant to ask. Captain Bartlett has a new set of furs, and I—

Peary: Captain Bartlett wasn't on the last expedition.

Henson: It's just . . . I might need new ones more than he does. Where we're going.

Peary: *(pause, then abruptly)* That's it. You all want things from me. You're all in it for yourselves. The Eskies want rifles, Bartlett wants the best sled, you want new furs. . . . That's not how it used to be. Do you remember? You were happy, honoured just to be chosen. . . . We were a team, we made sacrifices—

Henson: I'm ready to go, Sir; all I want is—

Peary: Where will this end? Not at the North Pole. We might as well turn back right now. I'll get a new team. There are plenty of able young men out there who would jump at the chance.

Henson: I just want you to treat me fair.

Peary: Fair? Matt, the Peary Arctic Club received a letter before we left. It's made me wonder about you.

Henson: What do you mean?

Peary: The letter was from Eva.

Henson: She wrote to you?

Peary: She didn't think you'd been very fair—

Henson: That is not my child, Mr. Peary. Not mine. Born in October! And where was I the winter before? Not in Philadelphia. No, Sir. She lied and cheated me; now she's cheating you.

Peary: We gave her $50.

Henson: I will ask for your money back.

Peary: She has a young child.

Henson: I'm not married to her any more. She was a liar and a tramp.

Peary: Matt, the Peary Arctic Club can't afford to go wasting money and time on all your frills and whims. We must have rules. We must have loyalty.

Henson: Ah, yes. The Peary Arctic System. Rule Number One: Take Matthew Henson with you. Rule Number Two: Don't tell anyone afterwards that you took him.

Peary: Then be happy I didn't. You don't have to tell them we spent all their money and didn't get there.

Henson: But I want my due when we get there—

Peary: If. If you get there.

Henson: A-ha. *(Pause)* You know the Eskimo are saying things.

Peary: They're always grumbling—that's their language as far as I can tell.

Henson: They don't want to go out on to the Great Ice.

Peary: They'll want our rifles, won't they?

Henson: They want to know where Qisuk and the rest are. They don't believe me.

Peary: Make them believe you.

Henson: I've tried.

Peary: Tell them I'll go without them.

Henson: You know we can't.

Peary: I'll get some other able-bodied men. They'd give their eyeteeth, you know. *(Pause)* Henson, please. I have a letter to write.

Henson: Is Bobby reading yet?

Peary: I'm not sure. He's six.

Henson: Then why are you writing? You can just tell him when we—

Peary: "When"? Think, Matt—

Henson: What do you mean?

Peary: What if—

Henson: What?

Peary: If we don't come back.

Henson: *(Realizing Peary's meaning)* Oh—don't say that, Sir.

Peary: We should have got there last time. I was a coward. We both were. We turned back.

Henson: We would have died.

Peary: We all die.

Pause.

Henson: I don't want to die, Sir. Not here.

Peary: If we're afraid to die, then why do this? Why? Just so we can say we were the first?

Henson: People can say anything they want, Sir. It's the doing that counts.

Peary: I said I would, I said I wanted to be the first and now . . . now I have no choice.

Henson: Have faith, Sir.

Peary: Faith? It's like some disease—

Henson: Don't say that, Sir.

Peary: It's got me; it won't let go. . . . Twenty-two years of my life, all sucked up, all wasted. You know that; Mrs. Peary knows it.

Henson: It won't be wasted if we—

Peary: If. That's it. If. If. We keep thinking if. If we can just get there, if we can just. . . . Enough. It's time to make an end of it. To see what everyone else can see. Head high. Chest out. Be brave. We're not going.

Peary picks up the letter to Bobby and rips it up slowly.

Henson: Don't—

Peary: I don't know why I—why we ever wanted to.

Henson: We want to see what no one else has seen—

Peary: We're mad, we're lunatics.

Henson: You planned it, scientifically.

Peary: Scientific lunacy! *(Pause)* I was trying to tell Bobbie why I do this. He made me see. I didn't know what to say. . . . Now I know: I'll tell him I'm coming home.

Henson: No.

Peary: Yes, Matt.

Henson: We can't go back like this, Sir. We have to get there. Think what they'll say.

Peary: They'll say, "Look at Peary. He failed." And I'll be brave, I'll hold my head high, I'll say yes, I—

Henson: No—

Peary: I failed—

Henson: No, they'll say, "Look at Peary. Look who he took with him. No wonder he failed." That's what they'll say.

Peary: But I've always taken you before.

Henson: They don't know that.

Pause.

Peary: No.

Henson: You need me, and—

Peary: I need you, I need the Eskies. That's the—

Henson: Yes, that's the system—

Peary: American science, Eskimo know-how. They know the terrain, they have lived here for thousands of years. We have to use their methods, their dogs, their food.

Henson: But think of the naysayers at home, reading their papers. They think they're better than the Eskimo— better than me—

Peary: They're not better than you, Matt. . . . Look what they do: They stay at home with their tea and shortbread—

Henson: They don't dare—

Peary: They're not brave enough—

Henson: They just stay home.

Peary: And say no, no, no. I told you so.

Henson: We have to show them; we have to go plant the flag there. Imagine, our flag standing there, fixed through the blizzards and the cold, for all to see—

Peary: If they're ever brave enough to come up North—

Henson: Like Dr. Cook—

Peary: Dr. Who?

Henson: Dr. Frederick Flannel Pajamas!

Peary: Dr. Famous Polar Explorer—

Henson: Dr. Hot-Water Bottle!

Peary: Dr. Charlatan!

Henson: Traitor!

Peary: Or the Norsemen. Yes, imagine them on their long trek, thinking they're better; they finally arrive, step off the sled. . . . They look up, and their hearts sink: Our flag.

Henson: We have to show them. We have faith. We're better. We can take it.

Peary: That's right.

Henson: I will keep these furs. I will talk to the Eskies. I'll make them want to come. If one believes me, the rest may—

Peary: The rest will follow.

Henson: It'll be like it was. We just need to convince one.

Peary: Yes, start with one—

Henson: Yes. I want you to pick up your pen and write to Bobby. Tell him why we do this. *(Pause)* We come up here to make our names, don't we?

Peary: That's correct. *(Picks up pen)*

Henson: And if—

Peary: If?

Henson: If we do not make our name—

Peary: But we will, Matt.

Henson: We can at least, at the very least, pass it on to some-one—

Peary: Yes, yes—

Henson: Who might . . .

Peary: *(Writes)* Make something of it! That's it. I'll give Bobby the most valuable gift I can. The parades and banquets all come and go; they pass. . . . Yes, but after that, no matter where he goes, he will have his name, my name, and people all over the world will know it: Robert Edwin Peary.

Peary Jr observing, flinches and groans.

Henson: Perhaps he'd like a picture?

Peary: Oh, yes. Will you draw him one?

Peary hands Henson a pen and paper.

Sleds, huskies, all that. He'll love it. I'm sorry about these, these lapses of mine. . . . It's the darkness—it just builds up in me. . . .

Henson: I won't tell a soul, Sir.

Peary: Only two more weeks, and we'll see the sun again. Thank heaven.

Henson: Sir, when we get back—

Peary: That's right, Matt. When. When.

Henson: When we get back, I may have my own son waiting for me on the docks.

Peary: You don't say.

Henson: Yes, I married a new woman now. Lucy's her name.

Peary: Matt, why didn't you tell me?

Henson: I did, Sir. We sent you an invitation.

Peary: Did you?

Henson: You must have been busy in Washington. It was just a small wedding. Coloured folk, mainly. *(Holds up picture)* How's this looking?

Peary: Very nice. Now how about a bear up there?

    Katie appears.

Katie: I want to see Qisuk.

Henson: Then first Qisuk must see you. Take off your clothes.

    Peary moves behind camera; they set up the shot.

Words and Pictures

The Eskimo Room.

Peary Jr: Mr. Henson—

Henson: You're interrupting.

Peary Jr: I saw your wife.

Henson: She's getting fat, don't you think?

Peary Jr: She's a handsome woman.

Henson: I think she's getting fat.

Peary Jr: She says they took your job away.

Henson: Does she?

Peary Jr: Did they?

Henson: They took everything, even the drawing I did for you. You ever see it?

Peary Jr: No.

Henson: You should have. It used to hang here in this room. They seemed to think an Eskimo did it. *(Laughs)* It was a bear hunt, I remember. There was an Eskimo on his sled, dogs and the bear was reared up like this. I put some igloos in, too, and up on the glacier, a woman walking. It was a good picture.

Peary Jr: Your wife says you don't have much money.

Henson: She always wants more. I was a courier boy in the Port Customs House for twenty years. Kept my uniform. Never had much. Never lost much.

Peary Jr: The family wants me to clear this up as soon as possible. I have an envelope here with a sum that we consider fair—

Henson: Let's see.

Peary Jr hands an envelope to Henson.

Peary Jr: We would require a complete retraction, explaining the real sequence of events—

Henson: My, my! You are serious.

Peary Jr: We will pay the same again when the article appears—

Enter Boas.

Boas: Mr. Henson! Nothing stops you, does it? Watch out— you'll be an exhibit soon yourself.

Henson: And then you'll want to pack me off, won't you, Doctor?

Boas: No, no. Heaven forbid.

Henson: I'm just talking here to . . . Commander Peary's son.

Boas: I'm Dr. Boas. I knew your father.

Peary Jr: Dr. Franz Boas?

Boas: And you must be Mr.—let me guess—Robert Peary.

Peary Jr: Robert Edwin Peary.

Boas: Number Two.

Peary Jr: Junior.

Boas: Now you have to rub noses with me; we eat fish eyeballs together and then . . . you sleep with my wife.

Peary Jr: Pardon me?

Boas: You don't want to sleep with my wife?

Peary Jr: No.

Boas: Now you are in big, big trouble, Mr. Peary!

Henson: Big trouble with Big Dr. Boas.

> *Boas and Henson laugh.*

And after you sleep with his wife, Mr. Peary, she will tell the whole village what you are like.

Boas: Then you, lucky boy, get to spend the rest of the winter with us. Fun and games!

> *Henson and Boas laugh some more.*

I'm sorry. It's an anthropological joke.

Henson: We're Eskimos, Mr. Peary.

Boas: Eskimos in the United States of America!

> *Boas and Henson laugh.*

Henson: Dr. Boas used to be the curator of the museum.

Peary Jr: Of course.

Boas: They've brought me back to oversee the renovations. Out with the old, in with the Jew!

Peary Jr: Things are changing here.

Boas: Well, we are trying, in our own little ways, to make it better. It hasn't been the most popular room in recent years.

Peary Jr: Do you still have all of Father's animals?

Boas: Oh, they're around here somewhere. Hibernating.

Peary Jr: He stuffed them himself. He was very proud of his taxidermy. Look, he'd say, just like they're alive. But they will last—last longer than you or me. So he thought.

Boas: They have lasted surprisingly well.

Peary Jr: Will they go back on display?

Boas: That hasn't been decided.

Peary Jr: But he gave them, gave all these things to the museum so that—

Boas: Sold, I think, is a more accurate term.

Peary Jr: I see.

Boas: They are our animals. So we will decide. Now, Mr. Henson—

Henson: I was telling Mr. Peary about the drawing of the bear hunt that used to be here—

Boas: Yes, that piece. We've had to remove it. It was unique, we thought. But we lent it to the museum in Ottawa, and they pointed out it couldn't possibly be authentic. The Eskimo never permit a woman to go up on the glacier alone. Especially not during a bear hunt. Malignant spirits!

Henson: Of course.

Boas: We won't be sending more artifacts to Canada.

Henson: I drew it, Doctor.

Boas: Good heavens.

Henson: I drew it for Mr. Peary here. When he was a boy.

Boas: Well, that explains things, Mr. Henson!

Henson: Then I saw it on display, and I didn't want to tell.

Boas: We should have put your name—your Eskimo name—on it. The bear hunt by Mahri-Pahluk! *(to Peary Jr)* And your father, the old fox, sold it to me. My, my. You're right, we never gave him enough credit, did we?

Peary Jr: But you say you knew him?

Boas: As much as anyone knew Peary.

Peary Jr: What did you think of him?

Boas: He was your father.

Peary Jr: But I didn't know him.

Boas: No, of course not. We must talk about this sometime. Now, Mr. Henson, business: You'll be here for a while longer? I would like to check some Eskimo words with you.

Henson: I'll come up, Doctor.

Boas: Let me come down. It's a pleasure to leave my little lair now and then.

Henson: Doctor, while you're up there, there are those photographs—

Boas: Photos?

Henson: You said you'd look for them—

Boas: Ah, yes. Of that Eskimo woman, your informant. They must be in the ethnological archive. I'll have another look. Toodle-doo.

Exit Boas.

Peary Jr: Mr. Henson, you know I brought you something else.

Henson: I don't want it, Peary.

Peary Jr: Well, perhaps Mrs. Henson would—

Henson: No. *(Returns envelope)* And you can take your money.

Pause.

Peary Jr: I know Father wasn't the easiest man. We'd just like you to help clear things up. You're the only one who can. There are all these strange reports and stories going around. . . .

Henson: Robert Edwin Peary—it must be hard not having a name of your own.

Peary Jr: What name did you give your children?

Henson: We don't have children.

Peary Jr: Really?

Henson: No, I've come and I'll go leaving nothing. Like the snow.

Peary Jr: Then make your wife happy. Take this money and give it to her. And set the record straight once and for all. Wouldn't it be nice if there were just one story set down and fixed that we all agreed on?

Henson: But you don't understand—

Peary Jr: Here.

Henson: *(Refusing the envelope)* I forget some things, then I come into this room and I remember other things. . . . It all swirls around me here. It's like setting off in the dark across a tablecloth that's moving. You can write down one thing, but then you read it and remember something else, things that were never written down, just spoken, drifting in the air. . . .

1909
Two Words

> *Henson and Katie lying down; they have slept together. Henson is mimicking with his hands the fall of snow landing on Katie's body.*

Katie: *(Laughing)* Qa-niq.

Henson: Qaniq . . . Qaniq . . . *(Touching her)* Qaniq!

Katie: No! *(Removing his hands)* Qaniq.

Henson: *(Miming places where snow might rest)* Qaniq. Qaniq. Qaniq.

Katie: No. No. No. *(Takes his hands and holds them suspended)* Qaniq.

Henson: *(Hands in air)* Qaniq?

Katie: Qaniq. Very good qaniq.

> *Henson's hands start to descend slowly till they touch her again.*

Katie: No.

Henson: Not qaniq?

Katie: No.

Henson: What?

Katie: Ah-put.

Henson: Ah-put.

Katie: Aput.

> *Henson's hands are on Katie. Now without removing them from her body, he moves them.*

No. *(She grabs his hands to stop them moving)* Aput.

Henson: *(Stills them)* Aput.

> *Now Henson starts to stroke Katie.*

Katie: No. No. No. *(Stills his hands)*

Henson: *(Touching and stroking)* I'm not qaniq, I'm not aput; I'm snow. Snow! Snow!

Katie: What's that?

Henson: *(Miming)* Snow on the ground, snow in the air, snow that gets everywhere—in your boots, in your eyes, in your food, in your furs—

Katie: Snow.

Henson: I am snow. *(Embraces, kisses her)* And you are the land in winter.

Katie: And when you go to the Warm Country . . .

Henson: *(Miming this on her body)* I melt away.

Katie: *(Laughing)* Then you are a very good Inuk. Just like Qisuk, Nuktaq, and Atangana—

Henson: You always talk about them!

Katie: We are a small people. That's what you said. And so I remember them.

Henson: In the Warm Country there are lots of people. They are very happy there. They are part of a big people.

Katie: Then they have forgotten us.

Henson: No.

Katie: Then they don't want to see us.

Henson: No, they want to see you.

Katie: Why don't they come back?

Henson: Because—

Katie: I know: Because the Warm Country is Eden.

Henson: No, no. The Warm Country is not Eden.

Katie: Then why do they stay in the Warm Country?

Henson: Because . . . Because there are lots of people for them to see in the Warm Country.

Katie: Look at me.

Henson: I am looking at you. *(He puts his hands on her)*

Katie: Who is Qisuk with? Tell me.

Henson: I don't know who your husband is with.

Katie: I know. He's with a pretty kabloona who has skin like milk, He's with Piuli's wife, isn't he?

Henson: *(laughs)* No, no. He's not with Commander Piuli's wife.

Katie: He's with your wife, isn't he? Is she a kabloona, too?

Henson: No. No!

Katie: She's a kulnocktoo, like you?

Henson: Yes. Kulnocktoo. *(Touching his skin)*

Katie: With dark skin and curly hair?

Henson: Yes, yes. Very beautiful.

Katie: Oh, Qisuk will be very happy.

Henson: No, no! Qisuk is not with my wife.

Katie: *(Laughs)* How do you know?

Henson: My wife doesn't have guests. It's not like here.

Katie: But you're away and she's happy?

Henson: Yes.

Katie: And Qisuk is happy? How can Qisuk be happy without a woman? He loves women.

Henson: There are lots and lots of other women in the Warm Country. Pretty kabloonas and pretty kulnocktoos.

Katie: I want Qisuk to come back.

Henson: I know.

Katie: He was as big, bigger than Piuli.

Henson: But he never went to the Big Nail.

Katie: The Big Nail! Who wants to go there? Only Piuli does—and Piuli's shadow. *(Touching him)* Piuli's big, strong shadow.

Henson: Piuli's shadow wants to lie down again.

Katie: If you lie down much more, the dogs will walk over you. After Piuli does.

Henson: I am stones, I can hold him. Lie down with me.

Katie: No. He will dig you up and take you. Like the Dog.

Henson: The Dog? It's just a stone—

Katie: It was a gift to the Inuks. It fell from the sky; the earth shook and hissed. And we had iron. Then Piuli came, and you came and dug the Dog out of the ground and took it away, and you took away Qisuk, Nuktaq, Atangana and the others. You took them away on the big boat, and you left a big hole on the shore. And ever since I have had a hole here. *(Taps her chest.)*

   Pause.

Henson: Is that why you go walking on the glacier?

Katie: What?

Henson: I saw you walking on the glacier yesterday when we were hunting. Inuk women don't walk on the glacier.

Katie: Since you came, the customs are changed. *(Pause.)* The Dog is gone. And Qisuk and Nuktaq. And Atangana, she's gone, too. Soon Akatingwah will be gone.

Henson: Don't say that.

Katie: And you will go, too. First, to the Big Nail and then back to the Warm Country.

Henson: I'm not going yet.

Katie: Will you stay with me? With Qisuk and me? You will be his guest, my husband's guest, when he comes back from the Warm Country, and we will go hunting together in the spring.

Henson: I will have to go with Commander Piuli.

Katie: Piuli, Piuli, Piuli! You really are his shadow. Soon you will walk like him, too.

Henson: Old two-toes.

Katie: What if he falls through the Great Ice? Will you go, too?

Henson: If he falls, I will come back and I will stay with you.

Katie: You will!

Henson: *(Teaching her)* And I Will Love You All The Day Every Night Would Kiss And . . .

Katie: Play.

Henson: If With Me You'd Fondly—

Katie: And if Piuli doesn't fall through—

Henson: Yes?

Katie: Will you push him?

Henson: No!

Katie: And if you don't get to the Big Nail. . . .

Henson: I won't go to the Warm Country. I will stay.

Katie: And we will be happy here. Very happy.

Henson: But if Piuli and I get to the Big Nail, we will have to go back to the Warm Country and be happy there. And we will be happy.

Katie: Will you take me with you?

Henson: You want to come?

Katie: I want to see the Warm Country, too.

Henson: I can't take you.

Katie: Then I will ask Piuli to take me.

Henson: Piuli!

Katie: He likes me. He likes taking pictures of me.

Henson: Do you like him?

Katie: I like the things he can give me. Ca–ra–mels.

Henson: He won't take you. He'll just give you his disease.

Katie: Then you take me.

Henson: But I have a wife there.

Katie: A wife! What does that matter? I want to see the country, I want to see the kabloonas and the kulnocktoos, I want to eat kabloona food.

Henson: What if you're not happy, if you're sick. . . .

Katie: Why will I be sick? I will see the Dog, I will be with you . . .

Henson: No, I will be with my wife.

Katie: Then I will be with Qisuk.

Henson: Qisuk?

Katie: Yes, my husband. He's strong. He's a good hunter. I will be happy. I want Qisuk.

Henson: I can't take you.

Katie: Then stay. Stay with me.

1935
Pick a Bone

The Eskimo Room.

Peary Jr: Mr. Henson, do you think President Lincoln was right? Father did, but sometimes I wonder—

Henson: What do you mean?

Peary Jr: Ever since the Civil War we've had all these Negro people coming up north. . . . More and more, going farther and farther. They don't find their kind of work, they're not happy up here, they end up doing things they're not supposed to.

Henson: Like what?

Peary Jr: You had a wife back home, a brand new Negro wife.

Henson: You've never been north. You don't know what it's like. Didn't your father tell you? Didn't he sit you on his knee in front of the fireplace and give you the whole story?

Peary Jr: I wanted him to.

Henson: And now you get me.

Henson pulls the drop cloth off a large object.

His sled. He thought he'd ride it into the history books, into the heart of America. Go on. Get on.

Peary Jr: I might break it.

Henson: It went to the North Pole, Mr. Peary. Come on. Quick. Dr. Boas is coming back to change the exhibits.

Peary Jr mounts the sled.

No, not there. You sit on the front—where your father did.

Peary Jr: There are dogs that pull us.

Henson: Lots of dogs, that's right, and they all follow the lead dog. You have to keep it in line with that—your iperuataq. Hi-ya!

Peary Jr: Excuse me—

Henson: We're off to the North Pole, Mr. Peary. Don't fall.

Peary Jr: I always wanted to go there, I used to think—

Henson: Head high. Chest out. Be brave.

Peary Jr: *(Recognizing his father's mottos)* He never wanted to come back. . . .

Henson: Don't you believe it. He wanted more than anything to return—the conquering hero on his dream chariot.

Peary Jr: So you kept going back—eight times.

Henson: He was never happier than when we left the ship—

Peary Jr: And cracked the whip—

Henson: And set out across the ice cap. Hi-ya! And the dogs yelped; their breath trailed like silver banners in the cold air; the snow squeaked. The world was new.

Peary Jr: Off you charged.

Henson: It was the start. Anything could happen. Mush!

Peary Jr: You drove the sleds out on the ice—

Henson: It cracked, it moved, it drifted—

Peary Jr: But you dared, you drove on—

Henson: Up and down the hummocks, where it had buckled like armour—

Peary Jr: Across the patches new frozen and smooth as glass—

Henson: Whooosh!

Peary Jr: You sailed . . .

Henson: Hi-ya!

Peary Jr: You had to go fast—

Henson: Fast, fast, behind us the ship's mast a speck vanishing—

Peary Jr: It was the past and you were the future charging ahead—

Henson: The dogs yelped—

Peary Jr: You were a team together—

Henson: Farther north than man had ever been—

Peary Jr: Full of promise for a new America—

Henson: We'd drink our tea—

Peary Jr: And look ahead—

Henson: We were a team, black and white—

Peary Jr: What deeds we would do together—

Henson: Together?

Peary Jr: United—Hi-ya!—in the new century that had dawned—

Henson: *(Abruptly)* Turn off the lights.

Peary Jr: What?

Henson: I'm asking you to turn off the lights.

Peary Jr: I thought we were going to the North Pole.

Henson: But we need help. Turn off the lights.

> *Peary Jr gets off the sled and turns off the lights.*

It's the Eskimo Room.

Peary Jr: There aren't any here, Mr. Henson.

Henson: They like the dark. Let's see if they'll come out. Qisuk! Nuktaq! Atangana! Where do you think they've gone? There are only two hundred of them in the tribe, and they live on a little strip of coastline between the glaciers and the sea, farther north than anyone in the world. Once they thought they were the only people in the world—the Inuit, the people, they call themselves—and that the world had no trees, no crops and, in winter, no sun—

Peary Jr: So it's dark—

Henson: Dark like this for four months. You take warmth from who you can. You eat what you have stored or what you can catch. . . . And sometimes you don't eat.

Henson picks up a box with bones.

Take a bone.

Peary Jr: What?

Henson: Where there's a dog, there are bones. Lots of them. Pick one.

Peary Jr: I want to turn the lights back on.

Peary Jr goes to turn on lights.

Henson: What would your father think? His son frightened like this! Look, it's dark, it's winter. I don't have much, but what I have I'm offering you. It's all I have, and you don't say no. *(Pause)* I'll have to pick one for you then.

Henson takes a bone from the box.

Ah, Atangana. Shhh.

Henson sets the bone on the ground in front of him and speaks to it.

Remember the Warm Country, Atangana? Remember? You came with Nuktaq on an expedition. You thought you wouldn't be lonely. But he only wanted to eat candy and pastries; he wanted to sleep with the ladies here; he wanted to sleep with Piuli's wife, with Mrs. Josephine—

Peary Jr: No!

Henson: Oh yes, he did. Nuktaq ignored you, ignored you till it was too late and the shivers set in. And the white men who were so friendly up there, the white men you pleased and warmed, here they were ashamed to be with you. Poor Atangana, you were here in the Warm Country, and no one loved you, not Nuktaq, not Qisuq, not the white men. But I have brought you back because there is someone here I want you to meet, who wants to meet you. It's Little Piuli. *(Laughs)* And he is littler than his father. He, too, is on a journey. He's lonely, he's frightened. I will give you to him now, and he will hold you and talk to you and keep you warm.

> *Henson holds the bone out to Peary Jr, who doesn't take it.*

Take Atangana. She's cold, she's shivering, she needs you—

Peary Jr: It's not her.

Henson: Yes, it's Atangana. Your father brought her here.

Peary Jr: Get that away from me!

Henson: All she wants is a little warmth. Take her. And let her take you to the North Pole.

Peary Jr: Away!

Peary Jr goes to turn on the lights.

Henson: Atangana, I'm sorry. Little Piuli doesn't want you, Little Piuli is frightened of the dark. I must put you away. There.

Henson puts the bone back in the box. Peary Jr turns on the lights.

Peary Jr: Mr. Henson, why do you come here? Wouldn't you be happier at home?

Henson: I like the dark.

Peary Jr: You like the dark, and you want to dwell on it. Gnaw on these old bones. Perhaps I'm wrong. Perhaps you belong up there. You should have stayed with that girl who wanted you. "Stay with me," she said. Didn't you hear?

Henson: We were on an expedition.

Peary Jr: Yes—and you're just like Father. He could never put it behind him.

Henson: He didn't want to disappoint his son.

Peary Jr: He went back time after time, squandering money, leaving us behind, and you alone went with him. No one else was fool enough.

Henson: I had faith, I knew we could get there.

Peary Jr: And just look at yourself now. Aren't you sick of it?

Henson: We did something. We pushed ahead, we planted those flags up there. Just think of them, think of the little boy at bedtime who lies his head on his pillow and sees those flags flapping as he drifts off—

Peary Jr: I was that boy, and I went to sleep not knowing where or who my father was—

Henson: That's what I'm showing you—

Peary Jr: You're going to disappear into the dark, like a shadow, and no one will care, no one will even notice. It must be sad not having anyone to carry on your name. . . . No one to guard, to cherish your memory—

Henson: We were going to the North Pole.

Peary Jr: I don't want to go.

Henson: We can't go back now.

1909
Departure

Quarters on the Roosevelt.

Bartlett: Harrigan, Ooqueah, and Poodlooqah!

Henson: Poodloo-nah.

Bartlett: I've got my Eskies, my huskies and I'm going! Hi-ya! Hi-ya!

Henson: What?

Bartlett: Tonight. The other parties will follow tomorrow.

Henson: Is Commander Peary taking you?

Bartlett: He's asked me to break trail.

Henson: I do that.

Bartlett: He's asked me, Matt.

Henson: He's always taken me before.

Bartlett: Up to now. Where's Verhoeff?

Henson: He's not eating. He thinks the tins are poisoned.

Bartlett: He's going mad, poor boy.

Henson: Do you think? Have you had a look at Commander Peary?

Bartlett: Why?

Henson: Look at his eyes.

Bartlett: They looked fine to me. Matt, me old cock, this is the moment. We have to seize it. Think when we get back—

Henson: If—

Bartlett: No nay-saying now, Matt. Just think how wonderful grand it'll be. Medals and prizes and special dinners, and we'll sit beside ladies in frilly dresses and answer their silly questions—

Henson: Certain people get invited to certain places. Others don't.

Bartlett: But Commander Peary will be invited everywhere: London, Paris, Copenhagen. . . . I suppose you'll be coming along later with the supply sleds.

Henson: Perhaps.

Bartlett: Bit of a change for you, isn't it?

Henson: It's the Peary Arctic System.

Bartlett: Seven tries. It's too bad you never got there, Matt.

Henson: We always got back alive.

Bartlett: I suppose certain people get invited to certain places.

Henson: Is that so? Have you read the Bible, Captain? Do you remember if there were any sailors in Eden?

Enter Peary.

Peary: So, Matt, have you figured it out?

Henson: What?

Peary: I asked Matt a scientific question a while ago, Captain.
. . . Where do women have the curliest hair? Think
about it, Matt.

Bartlett: *(Laughs)* It's dark, my son. Mysterious.

Peary: Jungles.

Bartlett: Waterfalls.

Peary: A place you of all people should know. Shall we tell him,
Captain?

Bartlett: Africa, Matt. Africa!

> *Peary and Bartlett laugh heartily. Henson's laugh*
> *is forced.*

Peary: You need a sense of humour on an expedition. That's
what I like about you, Captain. . . . I thought Mr.
Verhoeff was here.

Bartlett: He's not feeling well, Sir.

Peary: Would you find him, Captain?

Bartlett: Aye, aye.

Peary: Quick.

> *Bartlett leaves.*

Peary: Matt, we're leaving tomorrow.

Henson: Captain Bartlett says he's breaking trail.

Peary: I want you to stay back for now. I want to save you for the Pole.

Henson: Bartlett thinks he's going.

Peary: We're doing it differently this time. He's going ahead. But I'm taking you on the final leg. I want you rested up.

Henson: Did you cooney with her?

Peary: What?

Henson: With Katie.

Peary: I wouldn't do that to you, Matt. You've been so faithful to me all these years.

Henson: Commander, I'm not coming. I'm staying here.

Peary: What?

Henson: I don't want to go.

Peary: I said I'll take you. I will. I've always taken you before.

Enter Katie.

Katie: *(to Henson)* The kabloonas say tomorrow you are going across the Great Ice.

Henson: *(to Katie)* Tomorrow Piuli is going.

Katie: And you are staying?

Henson: Yes, I am staying. I've told Piuli.

Katie: *(In slow English)* Every Night Would Kiss—

Peary: What? Teaching her some new words, are you?

Henson: Just a song.

Peary: Well. Ready now to face the Great Ice?

Henson: I told you, I'm not coming.

Peary: You're not staying here for her, are you?

Katie: You can come up on the glacier with me.

Peary: Don't listen to her—

Henson: The Inuk say it's dangerous.

Katie: The Inuk! You don't believe those old men!

Peary: She has a husband, Matt.

Henson: She had one.

Peary: Don't start on that. There'll be lots of girls when we get home.

Henson: When? That's if you get back, Sir.

Peary: We will get there this time, Matt. Think all those years, and it's now within reach. Don't risk it now—

Katie: Tell Piuli to be quiet. Tell him to look at us now.

> *Katie embraces Henson.*

You will stay with me.

Peary: They'll like that story when we get back: Henson stayed behind to cooney with an Eskie!

Katie: We will be brave. You will be brave. You said you weren't afraid.

Henson: I'm not.

Katie: You will show me how you work all your kabloona machines, the telescope, the little stove, the picture box that goes poof! I will show you where to catch sparrows in spring, and you will show me where Eden is—

Peary: Don't listen! She doesn't want you; she just wants things from you.

Katie: We will tell Piuli he is not going to the Big Nail. He is going to stay here and work for us.

Henson: Yes, Piuli will work for us! He will pull our sleds up the glacier.

Katie: With his two toes.

Katie imitates his walk and laughs.

Peary: Stop your jabbering. Listen to me.

Henson: And we'll ask him to bring us the best pieces of food.

Katie: To give us his special kabloona supplies.

Peary: She's an Eskie, Matt. Don't be fooled.

Henson: We'll throw the scraps outside to feed him.

Katie: And sleep in his big bed, and eat his caramels!

Pause.

Go on. Tell Piuli to bring us caramels. I want some more.

Henson: *(to Peary)* You did cooney with her, didn't you?

Peary: A lot of people have, Matt.

Henson: You lied.

Peary: She wanted me.

Henson: She didn't want you, she just wanted things from you—

Peary: She wanted caramels.

Henson: She wants more now. *(Very upset)* Give them to her.

Peary: I told you she just wants things.

Henson: Then give her things. Go on. Ruin the whole tribe, Commander. Corrupt them all. You can't have slaves back in Washington any more, but you can have them up here, can't you? All you need is some candy, and they'll come running. Candy and a pair of blue eyes.

Katie: What are you telling Piuli?

Henson: I'm telling him to give you caramels. Because you like them. You like everything.

Peary: Matt, you have a wife, don't you? Lucy, that's her name, isn't it?

Henson: I had something, and you had to take it, didn't you?

Peary: Do you really think this Eskie feels for you the same way Lucy does?

Henson: So now you want me to come running, too? Like your little servant at the sound of a bell? What—for a caramel?

Peary: No, Matt. You're the best man I have. And I want you to be there with me. I want you—at the North Pole!

Henson: Then tell Captain Bartlett that.

Peary: I can't. Not yet. But it's you I want. Just think, we'll be the first, we'll see what no one else has seen. Who knows what might be there? We'll plant the flag and claim it for the American people, and when we return, they will give us everything we want: parades, banquets, fame. . . . Everyone will want to see us.

Henson: I want my due, Sir.

Peary: I will remember you, I promise. And you remember Lucy. She'll be there, on the dock, waiting. . . . And in her arms—who knows?—your very own child. Oh Matt, imagine: a son waiting to see you arrive. Waiting for you to give him your name, to tell him how you got there. . . . He'll want to hear it all. What will I say to him if you don't come? What?

Henson remains silent.

I'll start packing the instruments. You load and lash the sleds.

Exit Peary.

Henson: He's going to the Big Nail. And I'm going, too.

Katie: You're staying with me.

Henson: I'm going.

Katie: You are afraid, aren't you?

Henson: I want to be the first man to the Big Nail. That's why I came.

Katie: The Big Nail! You said you were staying. You were going to go up the glacier with me. Now you're not brave enough, you don't want to disobey Piuli. Then go on, be his shadow. That's what you want.

Henson: You went and lay with him, didn't you? Just so he'd give you some candies. You're like children, you people.

Katie: You say I'm a child! You played with me, and now you want to put me away like a toy and keep me from everyone else.

Henson: Did you have a bath with him? In his white tub?

Katie: You and Piuli are the same.

Henson: The same?

Katie: You think you own me. You think I'm a child. But I'm not a child. I am Qisuk's wife. And Qisuk wants me to be happy. Not just to be a shadow—like you.

Henson: I'm not Piuli's shadow. I want to go.

Katie: Is this the way you are with your wife? Will you tell her what happens at the North Pole? About me? What about Qisuk? Is he still in the Warm Country? Why doesn't he come back? And all those words you taught me—trains, railways, motorcars—they're all lies. How can there be such things? How? And then you tell me you'll stay with me. . . . I've learnt something now: I know you lie. I know that means you will go.

Henson: Everyone is waiting for me.

Katie: You're not brave.

Henson: I am brave. I'm going to the North Pole. And Piuli wants me. He's chosen me.

Katie: Piuli, Piuli, Piuli!

Henson: And my wife is waiting for me—

Katie: With your baby, the baby you want. Isn't that it?

Henson: I want my child to have a father.

Katie: He won't need you. He needs to be strong, to be a man. Look where he comes from. Piuli's little shadow, afraid to disobey, afraid of an old man who can't even walk. I used to like you; you were funny; you could speak to the Inuit. You could live like the Inuit. So I wanted you—and I wanted you to stay.

Henson: I want to stay, Akatingwah. I like you—I—

Katie: I said I wanted you. But not any more. Go.

> *Katie exits. Peary Jr walks up to Henson and lays his hand on his shoulder. We hear, perhaps, the last part of the duet from* The Beggar's Opera: *"If with me you'd fondly stray / Over the hills and faraway")*
>
> *They walk downstage. Pause. Curtain*

Act Two

1910

The Explorers Club

The Explorers Club, New York. Peary Jr, age
seven, pushes out his father Peary in a wheelchair.
In the eighteen months since the polar expedition,
he has aged greatly.

Peary: I'll tell them the truth.

Peary Jr: What's that, Father?

Peary: The one rule I know: Take. A gentleman's word is his
bond—no. Find a way or make one—no. Take. Take.
Take the North Pole. They don't know what it takes,
but I do. It takes a special man; it took modern science
and Eskimo know-how; it took meteorites and money,
yes, generously donated; it took lives, even American
lives, to reach, to conquer, yes, to take the North Pole.
I know because it took me. I took it; I took the prize,
(pulls a caramel out of his pocket) yes, only eighteen
months ago, I did, and now they are taking it from me,

Bobby. Yes, they are, in their meanness and envy. Don't let them do that to you.

Peary Jr: No, Sir.

Peary: Don't. Hah! What do you have that they would take from you?

Peary Jr: I shot a squirrel, Sir.

Peary: Have you stuffed it? No!

Peary Jr: I'm only seven years old.

Peary: Seven! If you don't stuff it, they'll take it from you, and they will keep taking for the rest of your life. That's why we have taxidermy, that's why we have photographs. Get your jackknife out and skin it.

Peary Jr: I don't want to.

Peary: They will take it from you, just like they took my prize from me. I took them there, I took America there, I took my coloured bodyservant, I took the Eskimo, and they were happy. Happy to take the salaries I paid them, to take the gifts I gave them, the knives, the biscuits, the rifles, the means of navigation. . . . And that was all well and fine. I didn't mind. But then it was not right what they began to take: my rations, my route, my caramels, my prize—

Bartlett enters with a bunch of roses.

Bartlett: Howdy!

Peary Jr: It's Captain Bartlett, Father.

Peary: Who?

Peary Jr: Captain Bartlett.

Peary: Captain Bob.

Bartlett: Commander Peary.

Peary: Admiral.

Bartlett: Admiral Peary, I forgot. Congratulations.

Peary: I apologize, Captain. Stiffness prevents me from rising. The arduous final trek. . . .

Bartlett: I was there with you, Admiral.

Peary: Of course, you were.

Bartlett: And now I'm here. The Explorers Club. New York City! Who'd have thought that I, Bob Bartlett of Brigus, Newfoundland, would ever be having drinks on Fifth Avenue!

Peary: Well, you won't. There's none to be had here.

Bartlett: Ah, yes, God Bless America. Look, I brought some roses for us to take to—where are we going?

Peary: The Grosvenors'. Gilbert's the President of the National Geographic Society. You can put them over there.

Bartlett places the six roses in vase on a table with a tablecloth.

They're all different colours.

Bartlett: I thought since I was buying six of them, I might as well get all different kinds. How are you?

Peary: Eyes still hurt. Scorched corneas.

Bartlett: And the nerves?

Peary: So you heard.

Bartlett: Mrs. Peary said.

Peary: It was my expedition; I raised the money. Six figures, a one with five zeros, one hundred thousand dollars— Bartlett? Are you listening? I was the first, the upright single digit, and they five shadows following, which when we returned, oh when we turned to come back, turned to crows, to vultures and took flight. They turned on me; they tried to leave me behind—

Bartlett: No, Sir. No, they didn't. They brought you back.

Peary: No, no, they tried to kill me. And then Dr. Cook joined them and the *New York Herald* and others, and they began to take more, take faster. They're on to my blood now. . . .

Bartlett: Admiral, Sir, have you thought—what are we going to tell them at Congress? Have you thought about that?

Peary: That jackass Verhoeff. They'll ask about him, won't they?

Bartlett: Yes. What an eejit he was, heh.

Peary: He stole a rifle, didn't he?

Bartlett: Yes, jumped ship and tried to run away to find gold. Imagine, gold! Then froze to death. Flaming eejit! We'll tell them that, shall we?

Peary: No, no. His daddy was a sponsor. We have to touch a chord. John Verhoeff was as sweet and brave a boy as ever trod the decks or looked for rocks. You were in grave danger, he jumped in, saved you, and little did he know, got caught in the ice. You grabbed his hand and pulled—

Bartlett: At great peril to myself—

Peary: It suddenly went limp—

Bartlett: A feeling I will never forget—

Peary: You saw his eyes imploring: go on, they said, for my sake, Bob.

Bartlett: He sacrificed his life.

Peary: That we might . . . that we might . . . what so proudly we hailed . . . tra-la-LAH-la-la-LAH. That's right.

Bartlett: They'll ask for your astronomical calculations and distances per day. They asked Cook for his.

Peary: Dr. Frederick Cook, the first man to the top of the world! That's what the *New York Herald* says. Dr. Flannel Pajamas, I trained him, taught him the Peary Arctic System. . . . And no one thinks to question him.

Bartlett: They have questioned him now, Sir.

Peary: And does he have answers? Astronomical observations? None. But the American public doesn't want to know about that. They don't want to know they've been had, don't want to admit it, that this liar, this impostor, this charlatan has had them all. . . .

Bartlett: Now, Admiral, you must pretend he's a perfect gentleman.

Peary: Ah yes, a colleague, a man of his word. Share the banquet with him. Would you pass the sugar, Dr. Cook? This cup I'm drinking from is awful bitter.

Bartlett: His story will fall to pieces; you must get yours right. Congressional hearings—we've got to be fighting fit. And they'll want the names of the Eskimo; they may want to question them.

Peary: The Eskimo? Yes, Henson knows them, Ootah and whatnot. I've asked him to come.

Bartlett: Matt? But I thought—

Peary: We haven't talked since. He's like a child really. With his hand out. Always wanting things from me. But he remembers the names, the details, and he'll give them to us, won't he? I told him I had a surprise. You're in town; we're having a drink—

Bartlett: Did you say drink?

Peary: Where there's a will, there's a way, Captain. For old times' sake. Bobby, you'll take Captain Bartlett down to get a bottle at Harry's. Like I showed you, boy.

Peary Jr: Yes, Sir.

Peary: Come back quick.

1935
Dr. Boas Returns

The Eskimo Room.

Henson: We met?

Peary Jr: Captain Bartlett and I ran into you in the street. He said, "Bobby, this is Matt Henson. He went with your father to the Pole." You shook my hand, said, "Mercy me," and we went off to Harry's.

Henson: I don't remember.

Peary Jr: Mother had sent me along with Father to New York. It was our trip together.

Henson: He summoned me to the Explorers Club. And like you, like a child, I came running.

> *Enter Boas with various sheaves of paper and a parcel containing a roast chicken.*

Boas: The pictures? Mr. Henson, I remembered!

Henson: You've got them?

Boas: I found where they are: the Department of Ethnology. Unfortunately, the creatures there don't want to release them. They feel the general public might not understand their scientific value—

Henson: But can't you—

Boas: I'm sorry. Down the road there may be some tricks we can try. Museums! That's what they're like! Dark, dark places. Full of warring and fearsome tribes. And they don't feed you. I've had no lunch. I thought you might want to share some roast chicken. . . . Mr. Peary, you're still here.

Peary Jr: I wanted to know what changes you planned—

Boas: May I eat lunch first?

Peary Jr: Here?

Boas takes the chicken out.

Boas: Please join us. We'll eat with our fingers.

They all take pieces of chicken.

Peary Jr: Like the primitives.

Boas: We're all primitives, Mr. Peary. Some tribes just hide it better.

Peary Jr: Thank you.

Henson: I got hungry waiting for you, Doctor.

Peary Jr: It's very good. I've never eaten in a museum before.

Boas: I want to bring life into this building, I want to make it live. If we make these things part of our lives, our rites, our appetites, they will come alive. We must find, we must teach people what we share with these Eskimos. No, we must be Eskimos, Mr. Henson—

Henson: Eskimos in the United States of America!

Boas: *(with Henson)* In the United States of America! You can put the bones here, Mr. Peary.

Boas holds out a piece of crumpled newspaper.

Henson: No, let's save them.

Boas: For soup?

Henson: Put them on display, Doctor. Remains of a typical Eskimo meal, circa 1935.

Boas: Yes. Note the arrangement they were left in.

Henson: There were three eaters. Two ate the drumsticks—

Boas: One didn't—

Henson: Why?

Boas: Why indeed?

Boas and Henson laugh.

Henson: Go on, have a breast, Mr. Peary. Your father liked breasts.

Peary Jr: You're mocking his work.

Boas: You misunderstand. We are all primitives—

Peary Jr: Come, Dr. Boas—

Boas: We all like breasts. This has been the argument, the entire point, of my scholarly work for the last fifty years.

Peary Jr: You're not serious.

Boas: I can only assume that you haven't read a page of my writings. Mr. Henson, there is a gentleman in Connecticut who has decided he is an expert on the Eskimo language. All of a sudden there are lots of words for snow, a veritable blizzard of paper blowing out of Hartford. Now, perhaps there are compound constructions—like we have in German—for types of snow, but I've gone back to my sources, and I can find only two distinct words. Two.

Henson: I see.

Boas: Two words means two roots. Perhaps two people, a man and a woman, say, from different places, came together and preserved both terms.

Peary Jr: Why do you think it's so complicated?

Boas: Because we don't understand it, Mr. Peary. Do you?

Peary Jr: No. Well, a couple of words—

Boas: We're talking about a place where a thing can have two names, a woman can have two men, a man can have two women. It confuses us. We make mistakes. *(Shuffling papers)* Here we are, Mr. Henson. Aput.

Henson: Ah-put.

Boas: Snow. And the other word is—

Henson: Qaniq.

Boas: They're both snow. I don't understand.

No response from Henson.

Peary Jr: Look, Doctor. Qaniq. *(Gesture)* Aput. *(Gesture)* Qaniq. Aput.

Boas: *(to Henson)* So qaniq's the verb "snowing," and aput's the substance?

Henson: Doctor, did you see her picture?

Boas: Who?

Henson: Katie. Akatingwah. She was young.

Boas: I don't recall—

Henson: You would have noticed her for sure. Very pretty—

Boas: Yes.

Henson: And she had a little scar here on her side.

Boas: I will get you the picture, I promise. Tell me what qaniq means.

Peary Jr: Look, Doctor. *(Starts to repeat the gesture)* It's snow that—

Henson: *(Stopping Peary Jr)* I'll tell him when I get the picture.

Boas: Mr. Henson, I need to define these words, fix their meanings precisely so we can preserve them—

Henson: Preserve them? Preserve qaniq? *(Laughs)* You can't catch qaniq. It goes, it always goes, it's gone, clear out of my head—

Peary Jr: What are you going to do here with Father's collection, Doctor?

Boas: Take it away. I'm giving it to you.

Peary Jr: It belongs here.

Boas: We're not interested in your father's trophies, Mr. Peary.

Peary Jr: You can't do this, Doctor. People will come. Just put Father's sled and his things on display here. Properly, with maps and flags and newspaper clippings. Appeal to people's sense of pride, of patriotism.

Boas: Is that what you think is right? For this room? The Eskimo Room?

Peary Jr: It's not just me—it's what the American public desires, what they deserve. But you wouldn't know that, would you, being a—

Boas: What?

Peary Jr: A foreigner.

Boas: An Eskimo, you mean? Did you hear that, Mr. Henson?

Peary Jr: This is an American museum.

Boas: And this is the Eskimo Room. I know what we will do. We will erect a scene from Eskimo life here. It will be winter, say, and very dark. There will be stars on the ceiling and an igloo here with a fire inside that makes it glow like some magic dome. And right here outside—

Henson: A bear hunt—

Boas: Yes, yes, imagine the bear, up on his rear legs, right here in the entranceway, his fur white in the starlight—

Henson: And above it, on the glacier—

Boas: What?

Henson: A woman watching—

Boas: Women don't walk on the glacier alone. It's a taboo—

Henson: Akatingwah did.

Boas: Really? This must be some new custom.

Henson: Customs change, Doctor.

Boas: We cannot have that here, this woman of yours. The exhibit must be authentic, Mr. Henson—

Henson: You want this room to live, Doctor—

Boas: The public will see the bear, they will feel what the Eskimo feels—

Henson: How can anything live here?

Boas: What?

Henson: People have died in this room. Don't you remember?

Pause.

Boas: There have been deaths.

Henson: I'm sure Mr. Peary here would like to know the story.

Boas: We can't dwell on these things, Mr. Henson.

Henson: Shall we just tell him that Qisuk is alive and very happy? That's what I told Akatingwah.

Boas: No.

Henson: What shall we say then?

Boas: You say it.

Henson: No, you tell Mr. Peary. Tell him what happened. You asked Commander Peary to bring back some Eskimo to help with your research.

Boas: I asked for one—he brought back six.

Henson: They were put on display—

Boas: And half New York came to see them, to cough over them.

Henson: But you couldn't speak to them. You didn't know the dialect.

Boas: So I had my driver go up and down Harlem to find you. We met.

Henson: They were sick, you said.

Boas: Influenza, pneumonia, whatever. No defences.

Henson: They asked for Piuli. "Why does he not come?" they said. "Why will he not take us back?"

Boas: I wrote to your father, and he never came.

Henson: Do you remember how they shivered? Right here in the little hut we made for them? And the first to die was. . . .

Boas: Qisuk. Then the others dropped like flies. . . . Nuktaq. And the rest.

Henson: Nuktaq, Aviaq, Atangana., Minik, Uisaakassak.

Boas: I wanted to stop the Eskimo and their culture from dis-
appearing.

Henson: So you did this. It was all for science, you said—

Boas: It was for science, yes. And for me.

Henson: For your science—

Boas: For my science, for my advancement.

Henson: And you advanced?

Boas: Yes, I did. . . . No, no, it wasn't science—just what these
idiots nowadays in Germany call science. It was our
tribe, their tribe, and bones. I killed them—

Henson: We killed them—

Boas: And I climbed ahead on their bones. . . . We met over a
corpse, Mr. Henson. You won't let me forget it, will you?

Henson: I'm just an old elephant; I don't forget.

Boas starts to leave.

Peary Jr: You want to throw out my father's collection and put
up this bear here?

Boas: Do the Eskimos have museums? What do you think,
Mr. Peary? No, we'll leave this room exactly as it is.
(Picking up a drop cloth) Think of these as shrouds.
Goodbye, gentlemen.

Henson: Goodbye, Doctor.

Exit Boas.

Peary Jr: No one will come. You need to show people something they can be proud of—

Henson: Proud? I was the only one fool enough to go back. You said that. And I did his dirty work for him.

Peary Jr: Everyone dies, Mr. Henson. Those Eskimo came south on an expedition. They weren't prepared; they perished. My father died, too. But he and you did something they didn't, something no one else did. . . . Didn't you?

Henson: What was that?

Peary Jr: Didn't you go to the North Pole?

Henson: There were six of us.

Peary Jr: I'm sorry?

Henson: Seegloo, Ooqah, Ootah, and Egingwah.

1910
Dark Race

The Explorers Club

Peary: Matthew Henson!

Henson: *(still speaking to Peary Jr)* But people forget, don't they?

Peary: Mighty good to see you. They're holding hearings tomorrow.

Henson: So I heard.

Peary: They want to hear the whole story. I'm sorry I never wrote back. I've been indisposed. *(Pause)* I want to talk. I've missed you. We were a team, Matt, weren't we?

Henson: We were.

Peary: Thank you for coming.

Henson: Sir, I'm ready to stand at your side again and tell those congressmen—

Peary: I'm glad to hear it, Matt. Glad.

Henson: I'll tell them, Sir, I will. Today the Explorers Club, tomorrow the House of Congress. Nothing will stop us.

Peary: I used to dream of sitting in front of this fireplace and telling the story. . . . Reliving it. Do you think about it much?

Henson: How could I forget, Sir? I wrote you letters, letters, letters. I wanted to remember it with you, to see if you remembered the same things. I wanted to be remembered.

Peary: Now, there were six of us, Matt, six. You, me, Seegloo, Ooqah and, and . . . what were the other names now?

Henson: Ootah and Egingwah. They were brothers.

Peary: That's right. Seegloo, Ooqah, Ootah and—

Henson: Egingwah.

Peary: Egingwah—yes, how he drove those dogs!

Peary writes the names down.

Henson: Hi-ya! Hi-ya!

Peary: And off we charged, a mad race across the ice cap.

Henson: Two sleds. I went ahead with Ooqah and Egingwah.

Peary: I navigated. We have to go fast.

Henson: Faster, faster. It's all or nothing now.

Peary: At the North Pole all the time zones come together. At the North Pole.

Henson: I'd stop and make tea with the stove that melted ice in ten minutes. I'd wait. Will the tea be made before you catch up with us?

Peary: Tea, pemmican, seal meat.

Henson: Eskimo food, furs, dogs.

Peary: The Peary Arctic System.

Henson: The American Route. We're making time like never before.

Peary: I'll get off and walk the last leg. Plant the flags there: Old Glory, the Navy League, the Red Cross, the DAR, my fraternity. . . . Yes, they'll like that, the old boys. . . .

Henson: On the sled, Sir. On the sled.

Peary: And my name I'll write there as if in marble: Robert Edwin Peary! Do you hear? Robert Edwin—what?

Henson: Stop.

Peary: What's happened?

Henson: Water. The ice has opened up. *(To Peary)* Remember that.

Peary: Black water. The Big Lead. We can't cross.

Henson: One day, two days . . .

Peary: Three days.

Henson: Four. Wasted waiting for it to freeze over.

Peary: *(As if composing)* As I waited and watched the white snow falling. . . .

Henson: Qanik. Qanik.

Peary: And melting without trace into that black water, I thought of—

Henson: Don't look too long in that water, Sir—

Peary: Of all the years I had spent in this endeavour and the many men who, preceding me, had not—

Henson: It's frozen over, Sir. And now there's snow on—

Peary: Snow on the ground—

Henson: Aput.

Peary: And fresh ice.

Henson: I'll lash the dogs. Hi-ya! Hi-ya!

Peary: I thought of Christopher Columbus, Ferdinand Magellan, Henry Hudson, Robert Edwin Peary!

Henson: On the sled, Sir. On the sled.

Peary: Ice—it's hard, it's cold, it's slippery, it's what we travelled on. And I have grown to know and love it. Come, look in my eyes: ice.

Henson: We have to go. We're getting close. You can write your books when we get home.

Peary: I, I, I want to remind you of the contract you signed. No lectures. No books. No interviews without my express permission. In the foyer, certain items for sale: Peary North Pole snowshoes, sleds, tents, camping stoves, tea sets. All tested in extreme Arctic conditions, on the race—

Henson: Commander Peary, get on the sled.

Peary: Of course, there were times when the men of the party disagreed, times when we quarrelled, times—

Henson: When I wished you dead.

Peary: And times when I felt the same.

Henson: But I remembered: You chose me.

Peary: I want to take you, Matt. You're the best man. Five more marches.

Henson: We're a team. You need me.

Peary: And you need me.

Henson: Four.

Peary: Three.

Henson: Two. Look, there's the sun.

Peary: We'll take a reading. Sextant.

Henson: Mercury. Artificial horizon.

Peary: It's eight miles in that direction.

Henson: Eight miles!

Peary: You'll go seven and a half and wait for me. We'll do the last leg together.

Henson: And so I went ahead, but the ice being what it was, I slipped and overshot the mark.

Peary: I asked you to stop.

Henson: I believe I'm the first man to set foot on the top of the world.

Peary: No, I led the party, I raised the funds, I navigated. The North Pole is where I say it is.

Henson: You said it was here.

Peary: I haven't calculated the ice drift. We could be forty miles short.

Henson: What?

Peary: Take the flags. Round up the Eskies and give them one each. You hold the Stars and Stripes, Matt. We'll find an impressive hump and take the picture.

Henson: Where?

Peary: Anywhere.

Enter Bartlett with a bottle and glasses.

Bartlett: We were detained at Harry's. Admirers, Admiral. They insisted on me telling them the whole tale, cod tongues and all. Which I did. Now, Matt, I reckon it's about time for that tipple we promised ourselves in the long ago. Bobby's downstairs playing marbles with the eyeballs on the bear rug, Admiral.

Bartlett pulls out bottle, pours drinks for all.

A toast. To the Pole you two conquered!

Henson: To the ship you sailed, Captain!

Bartlett: To the sled you drove!

Peary: To the dogs. The dogs.

Bartlett: To the dogs!

Henson: To the dogs!

They all drink; Bartlett and Henson laugh.

Bartlett: Hungry, Matt?

Henson: Come to think of it, I am. Are you?

Bartlett: I was joking, Matt. Remember dog pie? Dog stew? Huskie sausage? They ate each other; we ate them. *(Pause)* Do you two ever wonder where those flags you planted might be now?

Henson: You should have seen them, Bob, red, white and blue against the snow—

Bartlett: And now they're drifting off towards Greenland or Spitzbergen—

Peary: They're gone. Everything's gone to the dogs.

Henson: Sir, I'd be happy to testify on your behalf. I'm the only one who knows. I'll tell those congressmen.

Peary: Matt, it won't be necessary.

Henson: What?

Pause.

Henson: What do you mean?

Bartlett: Admiral Peary is taking me, Matt.

Henson: Twenty-three years, Commander, eight expeditions. You took me every trip. You said you'd give me my due this time.

Peary: Don't you know what it would mean to have you appear there in Congress?

Henson: It would mean that those congressmen, and that men and women all over America, all over the world, would know that I, a Negro, stood beside you at the Pole.

Peary: No, they'll look at you and think Look, Peary's brought his servant, his African, to testify. Monkey see, monkey do.

Henson: No, Sir. That's what you think. That's what you're saying. I'll tell them the truth.

Peary: They won't believe it. Can't you see, Matt? I can't risk it. They've taken everything from me. This is my one chance.

Henson: I got you there. I got you back. You were out of your mind. You were dead weight, you'd shut down, you couldn't speak. We had to strap you to the sled.

Peary: That's not true. I got there. I walked.

Henson: And now, you can't remember what it was like.

Peary: It was my expedition. I could have taken anyone. I made a mistake: I chose to take you.

Peary starts to leave.

Bartlett: Matt, we have no choice. We don't. We're doing this to prove that you both got there.

Henson: No, I never got there. I never will.

Bartlett: You were the best man. I know that now.

Henson: And now you're his little toady, his shadow, his nigger. That used to be my role, Captain. But I'm not doing it any more.

Bartlett picks up the roses and leaves.

This is the North Pole

Henson silent from previous scene.

Peary Jr: It's all a lie. Is that it? Father never got there. You never got there. You just pretended. And Father never told me. *(Pause)* He gave me his name and out into the world I went, repeating the family credo, off to silence every rumour, to parry—yes, parry—each malicious thrust. What choice did I have? Look at me: I'm like a tin soldier, all wound up and marching on after his death. Coming here to silence you, Mr. Henson. *(Pause)* It looks like I've done it.

Henson: Henson? Who's that now, son?

Peary Jr: Father never spoke to you again, did he? And you never got to the North Pole—

Henson: Shhh—

Peary Jr: What?

Henson: Can't you hear the dogs? Woof. Woof. Come, Mr. Peary. The North Pole!

Peary Jr: I don't want to go. I never did.

Henson: We're here. Look at the snow. Where's your flag?

Peary Jr: This is the Eskimo Room.

Henson: I am an Eskimo, and I can tell you this is the North Pole. Now you can make up for your father; you can make something of his name. Find a flag. Anything. It doesn't matter. This will do.

Henson removes a silk handkerchief from Peary Jr's jacket pocket.

Peary Jr: I just wanted to patch things up.

Henson: Come, Mr. Peary, plant your flag.

Peary Jr: Where?

Henson: Anywhere. On the forenoon of April 6th, 1909, after three centuries of attempts by men of all nations, you—say your name.

Peary Jr: I, Robert Edwin Peary—

Henson: Planted—

Peary Jr: Planted this, this handkerchief—

Henson: At the North Pole. The prize of three centuries.

Having considered various other spots, Peary Jr places the handkerchief on the large covered display case.

Peary Jr: My dream and ambition for thirty years. Mine at last!

Henson: Yours. The thing is it doesn't last. It's like a tablecloth, it drifts, it shifts—

Henson pulls on the drop cloth. Peary Jr's "flag" falls to the floor and we see underneath a display case containing a skeleton or perhaps just a skull. The two men stare at it. A silence.

Peary Jr: Who is it?

Henson: Mr. Peary, meet Qisuk.

Peary Jr: He wasn't a very big gentleman, was he?

Henson: Dr. Boas didn't want the Eskimo to disappear so he dried his bones and fixed him up. And look: an Eskimo in the Eskimo Room.

> *A woman, played by the same actress as Katie, enters the room through the same door as Dr. Boas has; she is carrying a load of linen.*

Woman: Oh—

Henson: Katie!

Woman: Mr. Henson—

Henson: Qisuk is dead. We put him here—*Qisuk tuquvuq. Uvunga ilivavut.*

Woman: I'm looking for the Doctor.

Henson: Doctor Boas?

Woman: Yes.

Henson: What?

Woman: Wasn't he here?

Henson: Yes, he was. . . . Akatingwah?

Woman: Mr. Henson?

Henson: *(whispers)* Oh dear Lord. *(to her)* Mrs. Chan, I, I—

Woman: I know: Daydreaming.

Henson: I'm sorry. I'm sorry. *(Pointing to her linen)* Is that for Dr. Boas?

Woman: He said he needed more.

Henson: He left a few minutes ago.

Woman: I see. *(looks at skeleton)* It's so cold. Why do you stay in here?

Henson: But this is the Warm Country. Come here, Mrs. Chan. Let me show you. *(Extends arms as if to embrace her)*

Woman: Watch out! I have a husband.

The Woman exits laughing.

Henson: Mrs. Chan works for Dr. Boas.

Peary Jr: *(Taking out a picture)* Mr. Henson, you drew a picture for me once. . . . Well, there was an expedition up to Greenland recently. They brought this back, and I brought it for you.

Henson: Is it Katie? *(Takes the picture)*

Peary Jr: It's a part of Katie.

Henson: It's not her. It's a man.

Peary Jr: And a part of you.

Henson: What?

Peary Jr: It's your son.

Henson: He's an Eskimo.

Peary Jr: Look. Curly hair.

Henson: No. Doctor said we can't. Tadpoles don't swim. Poor Lucy.

Peary Jr: He's got your nose, too.

Henson: The hair is curly.

Peary Jr: Who else could be his father?

Henson: I have a son? I have a son. A son. Well, well, I'll be damned.

Peary Jr: We were going to tell Mrs. Henson if you didn't agree on a retraction—

Henson: Tell her. Hell, I don't mind. This'll learn her. Matthew Henson, she'd say, you're pointing north, but what good's that pole? Never got me what I most wanted. Ha! Well, well, listen here. *(Pause)* Tell me. What's he like? What's he do?

Peary Jr: They didn't say. He lives up there—

Henson: With his mother, Akatingwah. Katie. *(He begins to laugh, to cry)*

Peary Jr: He must be grown up now. He probably has children of his own.

Henson: And their hair is curly, too?

Peary Jr: Yes, it will be—only a little less so.

Henson: Only a little less so. That's it—one drop of me already dissolving into their world of snow, one drop dissolving away in him and his children. . . . What's he do? I know what he does. He lives under the bird cliffs, hunts seal and walrus with the other men, and, yes, probably has a wife and children, one or two by now, and in the dark months, they huddle inside warm with their stores, waiting until the sun appears—

Peary Jr: Till the sun appears—

Henson: And spring begins!

Peary Jr: Here. *(Hands Henson the envelope with money in it)* Say what you want. Let people see the truth. We'll tell Dr. Boas to write it out on a copper plaque there—

Henson: Let's cover him.

Peary Jr: Don't you want everyone to see?

Henson: He's dead. Let him go.

Peary Jr: And Father led him, left him to his death.

Henson: Here. Take that end.

> *They pick up the drop cloth and very slowly settle it over Qisuk's case.*

Peary Jr: A shroud.

Henson: No, snow. Imagine that, a son way up there—

Peary Jr: Snow in the air.

Henson: Qaniq. You got children, too?

Peary Jr: Three. Julie, Susan and . . . Robert.

Henson: Of course.

Peary Jr: Aput. *(Starting to leave)* Well, I'll be late.

Henson: Tell them you've been to the North Pole.

Peary Jr: There's nothing there, Mr. Henson.

Henson: Shhh! Just say the North Pole came to you. Yes, it drifted right through this room.

The End

About the Author

Richard Sanger's plays include *Not Spain* (nominated for Chalmers and Governor-General's Awards), and *Two Words for Snow* (six Dora nominations); his poems have appeared in many publications, including *London Review of Books* and the *Times Literary Supplement*, and in the collections *Shadow Cabinet* and *Calling Home*. He has also written essays and reviews for numerous publications in Canada, Spain and Britain, taught at the University of Toronto and been Writer-in-Residence at the universities of New Brunswick and Calgary. In 2002, the Shaw Festival produced his translation of Lorca's *The House of Bernarda Alba*; in 2003, Broadview Press published his English verse translation of Lope de Vega's play *Fuenteovejuna*, commissioned by Soulpepper Theatre.